Toilets

Lynette Duggan

This book will help you find out all about toilets.
It explains about toilets nowadays and in the past and
how much more unpleasant they were years ago.

You do not have to read the book from beginning to end.
Just turn to the pages that interest you.

Contents

What are toilets?

A toilet is a large bowl which collects the waste from our bodies.
Some toilets use water to wash the mess down the drain.

cistern

seat

pan

joining pipe

waste pipe to the drain

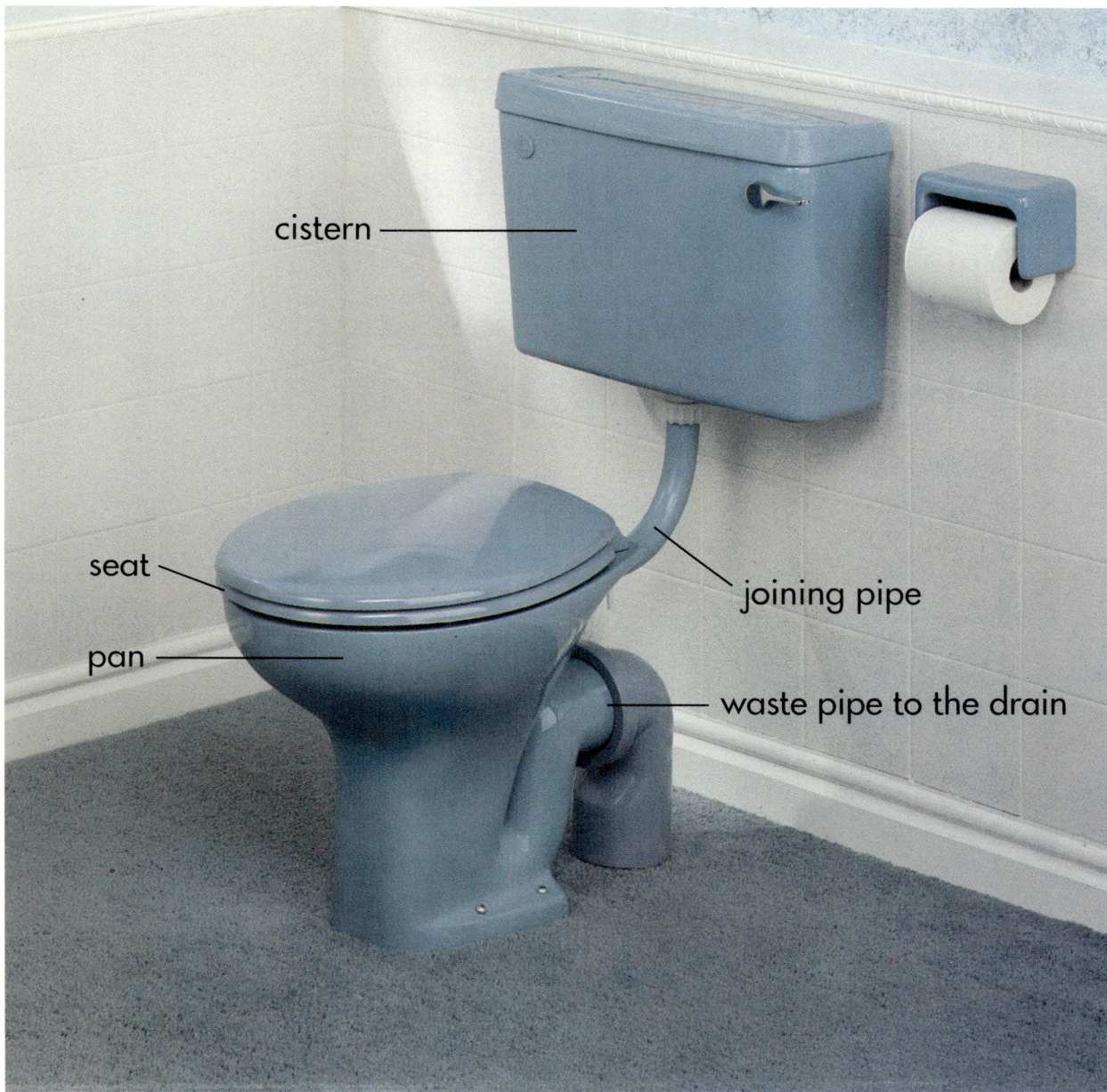

⬆ A toilet has a lot of parts.

The clean water for most toilets is kept in a small tank called the cistern.

Most toilets have seats. The seats can be made of plastic or wood. The toilet pan is usually made of a special sort of pottery called vitreous china.

How a toilet works

The water in a toilet washes the bowl and pushes the mess into the drain. This water starts to work when you pull the handle.

Fresh water cleans the sides of the bowl.

When you pull the handle on a toilet the water rushes out of the cistern very quickly. It rushes into the bowl and pushes the mess out of the pan, down the waste pipe and out into the drain.

The cistern then slowly fills up with water again.

⬆ Dirty water gets pushed into the drain.

The W.C.

Modern toilets are sometimes called W.C.s. This is a short way of saying Water Closets.

↑ This Twyford water closet has an oak leaf pattern on the outside.

Toilets were first called Water Closets because water was used to flush them clean.

Before water closets were invented it was very difficult to keep toilets clean. They were often very smelly.

Thomas Twyford invented one of the first ever modern water closets. It was displayed at the Great Exhibition in Paris in 1883.

⬆ Thomas Twyford advertised his toilets in newspapers and magazines.

The earth closet

The earth closet was a toilet without water. People used earth instead of water to cover the mess.

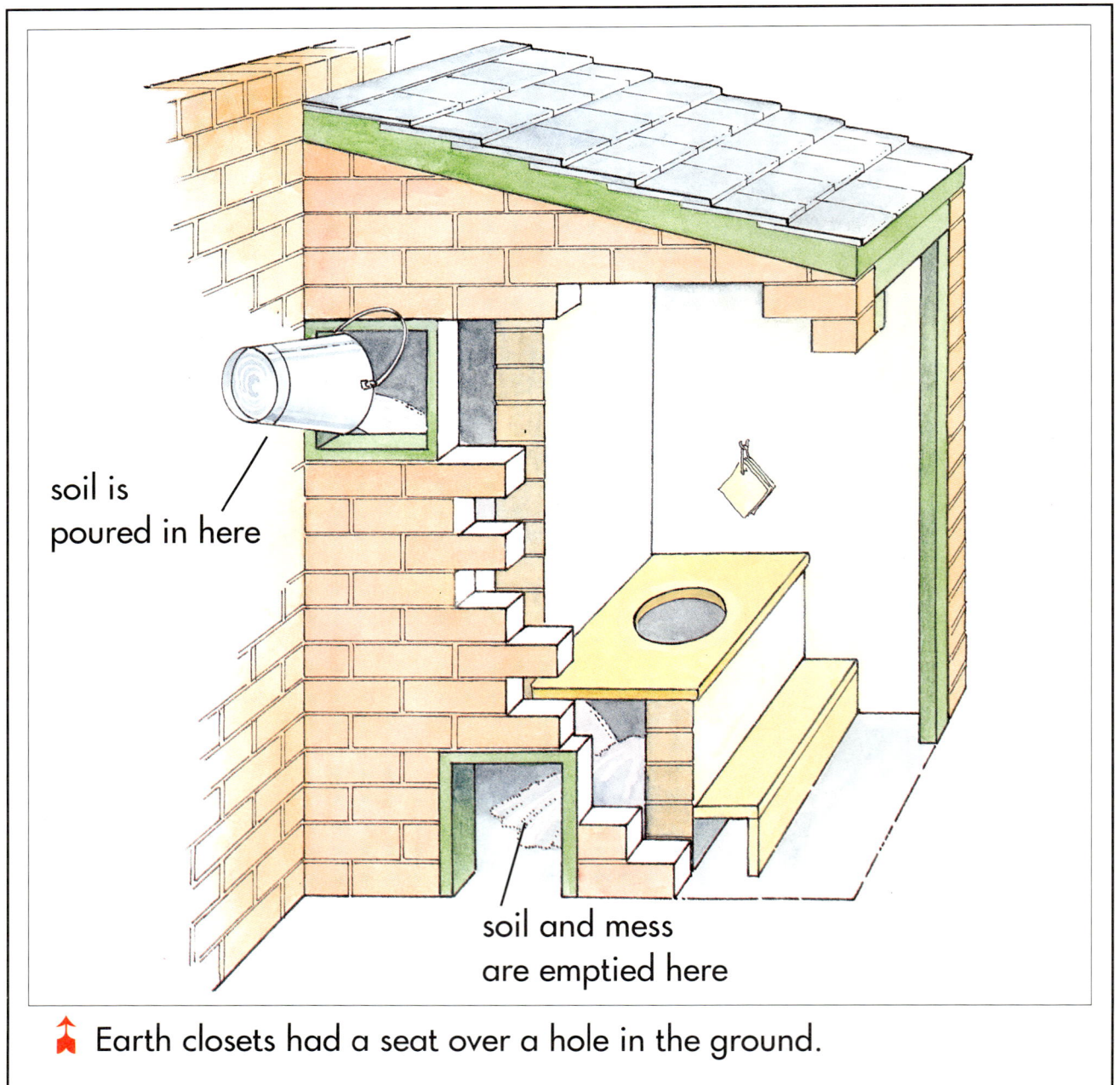

soil is poured in here

soil and mess are emptied here

🔺 Earth closets had a seat over a hole in the ground.

A hole was made in the ground. The toilet was put on top of the hole.

Soil was sprinkled on top of the mess which was dropped into the hole. When the hole was full of soil and mess someone had to dig it all out.

Most earth closets were built outside houses.

Pots and commodes

Hundreds of years ago there were no toilets inside people's houses. The houses did not have water pipes or drains to make the toilets work. People used pots instead.

Some pots were beautifully decorated.

Keeping pots inside the house was smelly and dirty.
Someone had to carry the pots outside and empty them
every day. Sometimes they were emptied out of the window.

Rich people used pots which were hidden inside stools
or chairs. These were called commodes.

This commode was used by Charles I, Charles II
and James II.

Toilets of long ago

A very long time ago some people lived in castles. The toilets in castles were called garderobes.

The garderobe had a seat built over the castle wall so that the mess fell into the moat or down the outside of the wall.

↑ This is where you sat.

⬆ The toilet seat stuck out from the side of the castle.

The garderobe was always built in a place
which was draughty. The wind took the smell away.
It must have been very cold sitting on the toilet
in the winter.

Travel and toilets

People often need to use a toilet when they travel.

There are toilets on trains, coaches, boats and aeroplanes.

🔺 This toilet on a train was used by Queen Victoria.

Most travelling toilets use water to help clean the mess away but the toilet has to be drained when the train or aeroplane comes to the end of its journey.

Toilets in other countries

In some countries the toilets are different.

🔺 This is what public toilets looked like in Turkey, many years ago.

Some toilet bowls in America fill right up to the top of the bowl before they empty the water into the drain.

In some countries there are squat-down toilets.
Many people believe these are more hygienic than toilets with seats.

Glossary of words used in this book

Displayed
When something is displayed it is put on show so that it can be looked at.

Drain
A drain is a pipe that carries water or mess away from houses.

Drained
When something is drained it is emptied out.

Draughty
Draughty means there is a cold wind blowing. You feel cold in draughty places.

Earth
In this book earth means the same thing as soil. Soil is the top layer of the ground.

Moat
A moat is a deep wide ditch round a house or a castle. Moats used to be full of water.

Soil
Soil is the top layer of the ground. Plants grow in it. Soil is sometimes known as earth.

Squat
Squat means sitting on your heels with your knees out.

Unhygienic
When something is unhygienic it is dirty. Germs can grow in unhygienic places.